AF257041

Accounting for Ship Owners

Steven M. Bragg

Table of Contents

About the Author

Steven Bragg, CPA, has been the chief financial officer or controller of four companies, as well as a consulting manager at Ernst & Young. He received a master's degree in finance from Bentley College, an MBA from Babson College, and a Bachelor's degree in Economics from the University of Maine. He has been a two-time president of the Colorado Mountain Club, and is an avid alpine skier, mountain biker, and certified master diver. Mr. Bragg resides in Centennial, Colorado. He has written more than 300 books and courses, including *New Controller Guidebook*, *GAAP Guidebook*, and *Payroll Management*.

Steven maintains the accountingtools.com web site, which contains continuing professional education courses, the Accounting Best Practices podcast, and thousands of articles on accounting subjects.

Buy Additional AccountingTools Courses

AccountingTools offers more than 1,500 hours of CPE courses, with concentrations in accounting, auditing, finance, taxation, and ethics. Related courses that you might like include:

- Accountants' Guidebook
- Fixed Asset Accounting
- Revenue Recognition

Go to accountingtools.com/cpe to view these additional courses.

Accounting for Ship Owners

Introduction

The world's merchant fleet of ships exceeding 100 gross tons is more than 105,000 ships[1], with more than 56,000 ships exceeding 1,000 gross tons. This massive fleet has a carrying capacity of 2.3 billion dead weight tons, and moves the majority of the world's freight. This fleet is comprised of many types of ships, but the underlying accounting is approximately the same for most of them. In this manual, we cover the essentials of revenue recognition, as well as the accounting for operating expenses, ship construction costs, depreciation, dry-docking, day-to-day maintenance, and several related issues.

Types of Ships

There are some differences in the accounting for ship owners, depending on the type of ship involved, though most transactions are approximately the same. Therefore, we briefly mention some of the ship configurations that ship owners may use, depending on the needs of their customers. These ship types include the following:

- Container ships (which carry the entire load in truck-size intermodal containers)
- Dry bulk cargo ships (which transport unpackaged bulk cargo, such as grain, coal, and ore)
- Ferries (which transport passengers and goods, usually over a relatively short distance and as a regular service)
- Gas ships (which carry liquified petroleum gas or liquified natural gas)
- Passenger ships (which primarily carry passengers)
- Tankers (which carry liquid cargo, and range from small replenishment tankers to Very Large Crude Carriers that can exceed 320,000 dead weight tons)

Revenue Sources

A common source of revenue for a ship is a standard freight rate, which is derived from the freight rate schedule used by a shipping company. These rates are based on shipping costs and the shipping company's desired profit margin. These rates are heavily impacted by supply and demand on the various shipping routes, and may result in altered rates on a daily basis. In cases where demand is soft and the supply of ships is too high, freight rates may be so inadequate that ship owners elect to lay up a ship for a period of time and wait for the supply and demand imbalance to resolve itself.

---

[1] https://hbs.unctad.org/merchant-fleet/

Another source of revenues is charter arrangements, which are covered in the following sub-sections.

Charter Arrangements

There are several types of arrangements under which a ship owner may choose to essentially rent out a ship to a contractor.

Voyage Charter

One rental possibility is the *voyage charter*, which is between two named locations. In this arrangement, the ship owner is responsible for operating the ship, and pays all of its operating expenses.

Time Charter

A variation on the rental concept is for the ship owner to allow a *time charter*, where the ship is rented out for a specific period of time. Under this arrangement, the crew obeys the orders of the charterer, who directs where the ship goes and what types of cargos it will carry. The ship owner charges a fixed amount per day, though a variation is to charge a specific sum per deadweight ton per month. In this case, the charterer is responsible for loading and discharging cargos, and pays for nearly everything other than ship maintenance and insurance.

Bareboat Charter

Another variation on the chartering concept is the *bareboat charter*, where the ship owner hands over the ship to a renting party, who must hire a crew and operate the vessel. This approach is most commonly used for yacht rentals.

Ballast Bonus

The preceding charters all involve the use of a ship in exchange for a payment, but that is not always possible. In some cases, a voyage must be undertaken in ballast, where there is no revenue-producing cargo. This is done in order to reach a port in which the next charter begins. In some cases, a charterer may pay a ballast bonus to help offset the cost of this voyage to the loading port; this only occurs when there is a shortage of ships at the loading point, so the charterer is essentially paying a premium to attract the services of the ship owner.

> **Note:** A large ballast bonus may be a way for a ship owner to avoid paying a commission to a broker, since there is no commission on these bonuses. This bonus would offset a smaller charter fee. We discuss broker commissions later.

> **Note:** A key contractual point is who has the responsibility for the loading and stowage of cargo, as well as positioning the cargo to give a ship a seaworthy load. Under a "net form" of charter, the charterer takes on this expense. However, under a "gross form" of charter, the ship owner pays for this activity.

Other Arrangements

Besides the preceding arrangements, there are several variations and addendums to these concepts that may be imposed. For example:

- *Fuel surcharge.* A ship owner may be contractually allowed to impose a pricing surcharge to cover any spikes in the cost of bunker fuel oil. This is known as a BFA, or Bunker Fuel Adjustment.
- *Long-term charters.* Ships with high capital costs, such as liquified gas carriers, may not even be constructed unless a long-term charter (typically of about ten years) can be arranged first. These contracts are periodically renegotiated to account for changes in operating costs.
- *Subsidies.* Some ships receive subsidies from the government, usually because they are being paid to operate on routes that would otherwise be unprofitable. This is a common occurrence for a ferry route.

Revenue Recognition

The revenue recognition processes underlying shipping operations are unusually complex, but still follow the basic GAAP and IFRS rules for contracts with customers. The following text is taken from the financial statement footnotes of one of the major shipping companies, which explains the matter in some detail:

> Regarding contracts with customers… the expected monetary compensation received… is recognized as revenue based on the following five-step approach.
>
> > Step 1. Identify the contract(s) with a customer
> > Step 2. Identify the performance obligations in the contract
> > Step 3. Determine the transaction price
> > Step 4. Allocate the transaction price to each performance obligation
> > Step 5. Recognize revenue when a performance obligation is satisfied by transferring a promised good or service to a customer at a point in time or over time
>
> … in recognizing revenue, we identify the performance obligations of liner trade business, bulk shipping business… and other business services, based on contracts with customers. In some cases, performance obligations are satisfied and revenue is recognized at a point in time. In other cases, performance obligations are satisfied and revenue is recognized over time by using an estimate of the progress towards complete satisfaction of the performance obligations, based primarily on the number of days within the performance period.
>
> [In regard to] matters relating to the five steps mentioned above, matters which [we] believe would be more appropriate to disclose by business segment are stated hereunder.

(1) Revenues from shipping operations (liner trade and bulk shipping businesses)

> In shipping operations… we provide customers with transportation services, etc. based on charter contracts and other types of contracts (e.g., consecutive voyage charter contract, contract of affreightment[2], contract for carriage of individual goods, time charter contract, etc.), in which performance obligations are deemed to be fulfilled over a certain period of time. In the case of transportation services (excluding time charter), revenue is recognized by using a reasonable estimate of the progress towards complete satisfaction of the performance obligations, based on the number of days within the voyage period. In the case of the time charter, since we are entitled to receive the amount of consideration directly corresponding to the customer value for the portion of completed service to date, revenue is recognized at such entitled amount.
>
> The transaction price depends on variable elements, such as the number of voyages, freight rate, demurrage[3], and dispatch money[4], etc., which involves variable consideration. The allocation of variable consideration charged for… the relevant performance obligations is achieved by allocating it to the transportation services in each voyage, because the allocation of the entire amount of variable consideration derived from each voyage to the transportation services in each voyage should reflect the amount of price we expect to be entitled to.

The financial report of another shipping company states the matter more succinctly, as noted in the following table extracted from its financial statement footnotes:

Type of Service	Nature, Timing of Satisfaction of Performance Obligations, Significant Payment Terms
Time charter arrangement	In case of a time charter arrangement, the Group measures its progress towards complete satisfaction of the performance obligation using a time-based measure. Further, because the Group charge(s) a fixed amount for each day of service provided, the Group has the right to invoice the customer in the amount that corresponds directly with the value of the Group's performance completed to date. Revenue is recognized based on percentage of completion.
Voyage charter	In case of a voyage charter arrangement including a liner, revenue for shipping services is recognized over time as the customer benefits from the service received as it is being performed. The Group identifies the performance obligation as the transport of goods from load port to discharge port. Thus, revenue is evenly accrued from the point of loading through to the point of completed discharge based upon the voyage days to the period end date as a proportion of the expected total days of the voyage.

Or, a shipping company might offer a multi-element arrangement to its customers that covers a variety of transportation and logistics solutions under the terms of one contract. For example, it might offer services covering storage and terminal operations, as well as inland transport. If so, this is considered a multi-element arrangement. Under the revenue recognition rules, the revenue from the various elements of a shipping contract should be separated into different performance obligations. The ship owner

---

[2] Affreightment is a contract hiring a ship to carry goods.

[3] Demurrage is a charge payable to the owner of a chartered ship because of a failure to load or discharge the ship within an agreed-upon period of time.

[4] Dispatch money is a charge payable by the ship owner to the charterer if a cargo is unloaded sooner than the agreed-upon time.

must recognize revenue for each of these performance obligations based on their relative fair market values.

Operating Expenses

Many of the operating expenses incurred by a shipping company are unique to the industry. In this section, we cover many of these expenses, including the characteristics of each one. They are addressed in the following bullet points:

- *Fuel costs.* The cost of fuel is typically the largest expenditure for a ship owner. Fuel prices may be set under a long-term contract with a provider, or the ship owner may choose to make purchases at the current spot rate. The price of fuel can vary by port, so a ship may sometimes divert to a lower-cost location to take on fuel. A further issue is that some areas mandate the use of lower-sulfur fuel within their territorial waters. This fuel pollutes less, but costs more.
- *Crew costs.* The cost of the crew is usually the second-largest expenditure for a ship owner. The crew frequently comes from countries with lower labor costs and a large pool of trained mariners, such as India or the Philippines. This cost includes overtime paid to the crew, which is usually incurred when a ship is being loaded or unloaded (though this cost may sometimes be passed on to the charterer). Another major crew cost is for food, which can be substantial, depending on crew size and voyage length. Many ship owners contract with a vessel management firm, which hires and trains the crew.

> **Note:** Employee turnover tends to be lower on tankers, where the pay is higher and employment is steadier. This is because a high degree of employee expertise is required to fully understand the pumping systems and handling characteristics of these cargos. The result is lower human resources costs associated with vetting and hiring new employees.

- *Repairs and maintenance expense.* The cost of repairs and maintenance is usually the third-largest expense. Ships are being operated around the clock in difficult conditions, so repair and maintenance activities never stop. This cost tends to be relatively low for new ships, and increases as they age.
- *Insurance expense.* The cost of insurance is usually the fourth-largest expense. This is a substantial amount, since a variety of policies are needed, including insurance on the hull and machinery, and marine protection and indemnity insurance to supplement the hull policy. It may also be necessary to obtain war risk insurance, which covers damage to the hull and machinery that was caused by pirates. Another policy is kidnap and ransom insurance, to cover the cost of negotiating with kidnappers and paying them off. Furthermore, tankers are required to have a protection and indemnity policy that gives the ship owner at least $1 billion of oil pollution coverage in certain regions.

Below these four main expenses are many additional smaller ones, which we cover in alphabetical order:

- *Agent fees and reimbursements.* Many expenditures are made on behalf of the ship owner by local agents[5], who submit these expenses for reimbursement – which is usually made within a few days. The agent usually assesses a fee for each ton of cargo worked during a ship visit, plus charges for other services not directly related to handling a ship or the cargo it is carrying.
- *Broker fees.* Brokers are used to line up cargos for a ship. The fee for this is usually 2½ to 3 percent of the freight, dead freight[6], and demurrage fees earned. which is split among the brokers involved in each transaction.
- *Canal and lock charges.* A ship will incur substantial fees if it has to pass through a canal system, such as the Panama Canal or the Suez Canal.
- *Cargo handling expense.* Depending on the arrangement, either the ship owner or the charterer will have to pay for the costs of loading and unloading a ship. In addition, there will be a charge for the handling of penalty cargo, which is any cargo that has been damaged, which is handled under distress conditions that precludes the handling of cargo by the usual methods.
- *Consolidator fees.* A consolidator firm may receive items purchased on behalf of the ship owners, breaking them down by individual ship, and using a freight forwarder to send them to a scheduled port of call for each ship. The consolidator also charges for warehouse space used.
- *Dispatch fees.* The ship owner may pay a dispatch fee to the charterer, when the charterer can load or discharge in less than the stipulated number of days; this is essentially a rebate paid back to the charterer. The charterer may not want to invoke this clause if it is cheaper to store goods on board ship, rather than in a warehouse on shore.
- *Dockage and wharfage.* Dockage is the fee for berthing a vessel at a pier, while wharfage is the fee to use a wharf to unload cargo.
- *Pilotage.* A pilot is always required to enter any port. This can include pilots who navigate around bars and jetties, those who navigate to or from the mouth of a river, and those who bring a ship quayside.
- *Piracy expenses.* Depending on where a ship is scheduled to travel, the ship owners may need to pay for armed guards during any transits through pirate-infested waters. In addition, there may be crew training costs on how to repel boarders, as well as the cost of a loss-of-hire rider to offset lost profits if a ship were to be detained by pirates.

---

[5] Local agents are needed to arrange for pilotage, towage, and cargo handling, as well as customs clearances.

[6] Dead freight is the amount of money equal to the difference between the freight paid on the cargo actually loaded and what would have been earned if the ship had been fully loaded; this arises when the charterer does not fill the ship to the capacity stated in the charter agreement.

- *Port fees*. Any harbor in which a ship is docked will charge a daily port fee that accrues until a ship's departure. This fee can be lower when a ship is only in port for bunkering (fueling).
- *Quarantine costs*. If a ship is declared to be in quarantine, then the ship owner must pay for fumigation and disinfection charges.
- *Terminal leases and operations*. A ship owner may lease space at a container terminal from the port authority. The ship owner may choose to contract for virtually everything, or may bring in its own company personnel to run operations.
- *Towage*. A ship may be billed for tug assistance. This fee can be avoided if a ship has bow thrusters, stern thrusters, and a dynamic positioning system.

Many ship owners will not bother to track the time of the crew as they work on specific tasks, since they are essentially a fixed cost that must be paid under any circumstances. A few ship owners track their time more closely. For example, they could track the cleaning cost of the holds. A dry bulk charterer might specify a range of cleanliness levels, ranging from "shovel clean" (the minimum) to "stringent clean". Similarly, the crew must clear the tanks on a tanker to remove wax and crude residues that might impact the flash point of such dirty products as fuel oil. This can be an extensive process, including a pre-wash, main wash, freshwater rinse, drying, and post-cleaning inspection.

Besides the preceding expenses, a ship also needs a substantial inventory of spare parts, which can be initially recorded as assets and later charged to expense as they are used. The amount of this inventory charged to expense may be relatively low at first, when a ship is new, but will accelerate as it ages. Also, some ship owners prefer to lay in a large stock of spare parts up front, when the manufacturer is still producing them. Parts are much more expensive later, when it may be necessary to build them in a special batch.

Ship Owner Departments

A ship owner could categorize its expenses by their nature, as noted in the preceding topic. However, it is quite common to categorize them by function instead, where expenses are apportioned among the various departments. Here are the usual departments that might be used in such a listing:

- Traffic department (responsible for finding the cargos to fill the organization's ships), which includes the following sub-areas:
    - Inbound freight (manages delivery orders, inland routings, customs brokers, warehousing, and claims)
    - General delivery agent (includes sales staff, administration, and the statistical staff)
    - Outbound freight (manages bookings, vessel clearances and cargo manifests)

- Operations department (responsible for ship construction, operations, cargo handling, and labor relations), which includes the following areas of responsibility:

  o Marine superintendent (manages deck personnel, inspections, and safety)
  o Superintendent engineer (manages engineering, maintenance and repairs)
  o Commissary superintendent (manages stewards, requisitions, and inventories)
  o Purchasing agent (manages purchasing, inventories of stores and equipment, and spare parts)
  o Terminal manager (manages receiving and delivery, cargo handling, security, administration, and custodial care)

Accounting for the Financing of Ship Construction

Ships are extremely expensive to build, so they are mostly financed by lenders, which use the hull as collateral. The lenders insist on comprehensive insurance coverage on these ships, since this constitutes a backup payment plan in case a ship is damaged or sunk.

The shipyard cannot self-finance the cost of a ship, so it bills the ship owner at certain milestones for a set percentage of the total price of a ship. This commonly mandates a 15% to 20% billing at the time of order placement, along with additional payments as certain milestones are reached.

Ship Purchase Commitments

The number of shipyards at which ships (especially very large ones) can be built is limited, so shipowners have to enter into long-term purchase commitments in order to lock in a slot at a shipyard. In addition, a shipowner may purchase an option to acquire additional ships, thereby locking in a price and delivery slot. Given the size of these commitments, a shipowner should describe the extent of these commitments in the footnotes to its financial statements.

It is sometimes possible for a ship owner to acquire a construction option on the secondary market. If so, the purchase price of the option is treated as a prepayment on the construction cost of the vessel, and would appear as an asset on the ship owner's balance sheet.

Ship Construction Costs

There are numerous costs associated with constructing a ship and then putting it into service. Here are the most likely costs that a ship owner will incur:

- The cost of any purchase options needed for the vessel

- Predelivery installment payments to the shipbuilding yard for ship construction
- Financing costs
- Vehicle registration and certification costs
- Seaworthiness certificates
- Legal costs linked to the ship purchase
- The costs to bring the ship to the location and condition needed for it to become operational

The predelivery installment payments to the shipyard are initially recorded as prepayments, and are classified as a non-current asset. Once the associated vessel is delivered, these prepayments are included in the cost of the asset.

Any financing costs incurred by the ship owner for the construction of the vessel are to be capitalized into its cost. The amount of interest cost to capitalize is that amount of interest that would have been avoided if the vessel had not been acquired. The capitalization of these costs should cease as soon as the associated vessel has been substantially completed. However, if there are prolonged periods during which no work is being conducted on a vessel (such as during a shipyard strike by workers), no financing costs should be capitalized during these periods. If some of the funds borrowed for construction are invested for a period of time before being used on the vessel, the interest income on the invested funds should offset the capitalized amount of interest.

The basis for the capitalization rate is the interest rates that are applicable to the ship owner's borrowings that are outstanding during the construction period. If a specific borrowing is incurred in order to construct a vessel, use the interest rate on that borrowing as the capitalization rate. If the amount of a specific borrowing that is incurred to construct an asset is less than the expenditures made for the asset, use a weighted average of the rates applicable to other company borrowings for any excess expenditures over the amount of the vessel-specific borrowing.

A number of expenditures can be included in the cost to bring a vessel to the location and condition needed for it to become operational. For example, the ship owner may need to pay staff to operate the vessel during its sea trials, as well as for the bunker fuel consumed by the vessel during those trials.

The other costs noted in the preceding bullet points should be recorded in the Vessels Under Construction account, which is a fixed asset account. Once the ship owner has taken delivery of a vessel and made final payments for it, the aggregate amount is shifted out of the Vessels Under Construction account and shifted into a separate, unique fixed asset account.

EXAMPLE

Rio Shipping contracts with a shipyard to build it a bulk carrier. The contract price is $60 million, with the following terms:

Milestones	Milestone Dates	Percentage Paid	Amount Paid
Contract signing	February 1, 20X1	15% of contract total	$9,000,000
Steel cutting	October 1, 20X1	35% of contract total	21,000,000
Keel laying	January 1, 20X2	20% of contract total	12,000,000
Delivery	November 1, 20X2	30% of contract total	18,000,000
Total			$60,000,000

Rio takes out a loan at a 6.5% interest rate, which it draws upon at each of the milestone dates to pay for the milestone requirements. The vessel will undergo two months of sea trials following its November 1 delivery, and so will be expected to be in service by December 31, 20X2.

Rio also incurs the following costs relating to the construction of the bulk carrier:

- $1,800,000 Broker's commission (at 3% of contract price)
- $10,000 Legal fees to establish title
- $70,000 Supervisory costs
- $10,000 Travel costs
- $20,000 Vessel inspection costs

All of these added costs, totaling $1,910,000, should be capitalized into the cost of the vessel, since they are directly related to this asset, and would not have been incurred if the vessel had not been purchased. When added to the $60 million of milestone payments made for the vessel, these additional capitalizations increase its capitalized cost to $61,910,000.

In addition, Rio must capitalize the cost of the interest incurred as a result of this vessel acquisition. The interest capitalization calculation is as follows:

Payment Tranche	Calculation	Interest to Capitalize
Contract signing milestone	$9,000,000 × 6.5% × 23/12 months	$1,121,250
Steel cutting milestone	$21,000,000 × 6.5% × 15/12 months	1,706,250
Keel laying milestone	$12,000,000 × 6.5% × 12/12 months	780,000
Delivery milestone	$18,000,000 × 6.5% × 2/12 months	195,000
Total		$3,802,500

Therefore, the capitalized cost of the bulk carrier will be $61,910,000 + $3,802,500 of capitalized interest, for a total capitalized cost of $65,712,500.

Ship Depreciation Issues

A vessel must be depreciated over its useful life. The related accounting is not so simple, since various components of the vessel have different useful lives, and so must be depreciated separately. This is not the case for a vessel's engines, which generally cannot be replaced before the useful life of the hull has ended. Consequently, the hull and engines are depreciated over the same time period.

The useful life of a ship is a determination made by the ship owner, so there is some variation in the periods used. Typically, a tanker ship will be assigned a useful life of 25 years, while container and dry-bulk ships may be assigned slightly longer lives, perhaps extending out as far as 30 years.

The salvage value of a vessel is usually considered to be its scrap value. This value is derived by calculating the number of tons of steel within it, and multiplying this value by the market rate for scrap steel. The resulting scrap proceeds must then be reduced by the costs expected to be incurred to scrap the vessel. These costs should include the costs to be incurred to move the vessel to a scrap yard.

The standard depreciation method used by most ship owners is the straight-line method. Under this method, you should recognize depreciation expense evenly over the estimated useful life of an asset. The straight-line calculation steps are:

1. Subtract the estimated salvage value of the asset from the amount at which it is recorded on the books.
2. Determine the estimated useful life of the asset. It is easiest to use a standard useful life for each class of assets.
3. Divide the estimated useful life (in years) into 1 to arrive at the straight-line depreciation rate.
4. Multiply the depreciation rate by the asset cost (less salvage value).

EXAMPLE

Rocker Corporation takes delivery of a tanker, for which it paid $40 million. It has an estimated salvage value of $5 million and a useful life of 25 years. Rocker calculates the annual straight-line depreciation for the tanker as:

1. Purchase cost of $40 million – Estimated salvage value of $5 million = Depreciable asset cost of $35 million
2. 1 ÷ 25-Year useful life = 4% Depreciation rate per year
3. 4% Depreciation rate × $35 Million depreciable asset cost = $1.4 Million annual depreciation

---

Given the extremely large vessel costs incurred by a ship owner, any changes in the estimated useful life or salvage value of a vessel could have a material impact on its depreciation expense. Consequently, it would be prudent to review the useful life and salvage estimates on at least an annual basis. If changes are made to these estimates, the change is made prospectively, over the remaining life of the vessel. This means that the depreciation recognized in prior periods would not be impacted.

Accounting for Dry-Docking Maintenance

All ships used for commercial operations are required to go into dry-dock at regular intervals. Dry-docking involves a standard, periodic overhaul[7] (usually every three to five years), which can cost anywhere in the range of hundreds of thousands to millions of dollars. In dry-docking, a ship is removed from the water so that it can be thoroughly inspected and repaired, including all areas that would normally be below the waterline. A complete overhaul will definitely extend the useful life of a ship, since it involves extensive maintenance work on the hull, engines, main deck, compressors, turbines, pumps, and so forth.

The proper accounting for the cost of a dry-docking is to capitalize its cost, and then depreciate it through the period until the next scheduled overhaul. This approach appropriately spreads the cost of dry-docking over the benefit period, which ends when the next dry-docking begins.

EXAMPLE

Rio Shipping purchases a cargo ship for $50 million, which it plans to use for the next 30 years, at which point it will have a scrap value of $1 million. The owners decide that $3 million of the vessel's components will be replaced at the next dry-docking, which is scheduled for five years in the future. This results in the following annual depreciation calculations:

Asset type	Cost	Useful Life	Salvage Value	Annual Depreciation
Vessel, less dry-dock component replacements	$47,000,000	30 years	$1,000,000	$1,533,333
Dry-dock component replacements	3,000,000	5 years	0	600,000
	$50,000,000			$2,133,333

An implication of this accounting treatment is that all components of a vessel that will be replaced at the next dry-docking interval should be identified and tracked separately in the accounting records, using a depreciation method that ensures that they will be completely depreciated by the time of the next scheduled dry-docking.

A further implication of the need to identify those assets that will be replaced at the next dry-docking is that the rest of the vessel's cost should be identified and accounted for separately, as of the date when the ship owner initially takes delivery of the vessel.

---

[7] A dry-dock overhaul may include hull cleaning and painting, the examination of the rudder, tail shaft, propeller, anchors and chains, ballast tanks, cargo holds, hatches, cranes, piping, main machinery, deck machinery, pumps, batteries, wiring, and compressors.

> **Tip:** It can be difficult to identify at the point of vessel delivery those assets that will be replaced at the next dry-docking, and those that will not. Consequently, you may need to determine the fair value of each of these components, and assign costs to the various assets on that basis. Fair value information can be obtained from appraisers or other specialists.

If, as part of the dry-docking procedure, the maintenance staff finds that additional items must be replaced (such as a complete engine replacement), then you should de-recognize the carrying amount of the old asset and capitalize the cost of the replacement asset. The cost of the replacement asset should be depreciated over the estimated useful life of the asset, which may cover a longer period than the interval to the next dry-docking.

> **Note:** There will be more expenditures on a vessel as it ages, which means that the cost of each successive dry-docking will increase. This will necessarily result in an ongoing and gradual increase in the depreciation charge from one year to the next.

Accounting for Day-to-Day Maintenance

A ship owner will likely need to pay for a substantial amount of day-to-day maintenance work on its vessels. When this maintenance work does not materially enhance an asset, then the cost of the maintenance is charged to expense as incurred. However, if the maintenance work replaces a component, then the component that was replaced should be accounted for as having been disposed of, with the replacement being accounted for as a replacement asset.

In most cases, major maintenance will have been planned for, so that the useful life of a component will align with the maintenance intervals at which the component is expected to be replaced. This means that the associated book value of a component should be near zero by the time it is scheduled for replacement. If this is not the case, and there is still some book value left, this amount should be charged to expense as soon as the replacement is completed.

If a component was not initially tracked separately from the main vessel asset and is later replaced, you will need to estimate what the current book value of the component would be, as though it had initially been carved out as a separate asset. This may require you to determine the component's initial cost based on its replacement cost, from which a depreciation charge is deducted that uses the depreciation rate used for the rest of the hull. This will likely result in a significant carrying amount for the component, which must then be charged to expense as soon as the replacement has been installed.

Accounting for Intermediate and Special Surveys

A ship owner is required to conduct periodic intermediate[8] and special surveys of a vessel over the course of its useful life, in addition to dry-docking. For example, a special survey may be needed every five years, with an intermediate survey being conducted in-between. The cost of each of these surveys can be capitalized, and depreciated until the next scheduled survey.

Vessel Impairment Testing

A basic rule of accounting is that you should recognize an impairment loss on a fixed asset if its carrying amount is not recoverable and exceeds its fair value. The carrying amount of an asset is not recoverable if it exceeds the sum of the undiscounted cash flows expected to result from the use of the asset over its remaining useful life and the final disposition of the asset. In developing a cash flow model for this analysis, most ship owners have no trouble determining cash outflows, since they routinely analyze the daily operating costs of their ships. However, it is much more difficult to estimate cash inflows, since freight rates can vary wildly, depending on economic conditions and unusual events (such as the closure of the Suez Canal due to a blockage, or terrorist attacks in the Red Sea).

Impairment testing is a major issue for ship owners, since they have an enormous investment in vessels, which are subject to impairment. Consequently, it is critical to conduct accurate impairment tests on them. An improperly conducted impairment test could have a substantial impact on a firm's reported profits.

You should test for the recoverability of an asset whenever the circumstances indicate that its carrying amount may not be recoverable. Examples of such situations are:

- *Cash flow.* There are historical and projected operating or cash flow losses associated with the asset.
- *Costs.* There are excessive costs incurred to acquire or construct the asset.
- *Disposal.* The asset is more than 50% likely to be sold or otherwise disposed of significantly before the end of its previously estimated useful life.
- *Legal.* There is a significant adverse change in legal factors or the business climate that could affect the asset's value.
- *Market price.* There is a significant decrease in the asset's market price.
- *Usage.* There is a significant adverse change in the asset's manner of use, or in its physical condition.

The amount of an impairment loss is the difference between an asset's carrying amount and its fair value. Once you recognize an impairment loss, this reduces the carrying amount of the asset, so you may need to alter the amount of periodic depreciation being charged against the asset to adjust for this lower carrying amount

---

[8] An intermediate inspection is conducted between the second or third year between dry-docking, where the scope of the inspection depends on the age of the vessel.

(otherwise, you will incur an excessively large depreciation expense over the remaining useful life of the asset).

EXAMPLE

Rio Shipping finds that a worldwide glut in the market for supertankers has reduced the usage level of its Rio Sunrise supertanker by 10 percent. This does not translate into a sufficient drop in the cash flows or market value of the ship to warrant an impairment charge. Nonetheless, Rio's management is concerned that the glut could continue for many years to come, and so it alters the depreciation method for the supertanker from the straight-line method to the 150% declining balance method, in order to accelerate depreciation and reduce the carrying amount of the asset more quickly. This will reduce the risk of having to incur an impairment charge at a later date.

It can be difficult to ascertain the fair value of a ship, because it is based on a mix of construction costs and the supply of and demand for ships. In addition, the demand for a new ship is largely based on ship owners' expectations for long-term demand, while the demand for used ships is largely based on short-term demand expectations. In addition, the supply side of the equation will depend on whether there are new vessels being constructed in an asset class that might negatively impact the values of existing vessels in the same class. A further consideration is whether the maintenance condition of a vessel varies substantially from the average maintenance condition of the other vessels in its asset class; if so, this may call for an adjustment in the presumed fair value of the vessel.

> **Note:** Freight rates definitely go through a cycle, where the oversupply of ships or weakened demand leads to a collapse in rates. At this point in the industry cycle, ship owners are more likely to retire those ships with high maintenance costs – which leads to considerable impairment charges.

EXAMPLE

Rio Shipping owns a small coastal freighter with an original cost of $14 million and estimated salvage value of $4 million, and which it has been depreciating on the straight-line basis for five years. The freighter now has a carrying amount of $9 million.

Rio conducts an impairment test of the freighter asset, and concludes that the fair value less cost to sell of the asset is much lower than original estimates, resulting in a recoverable amount of $7 million. Rio takes a $2 million impairment charge to reduce the carrying amount of the freighter from $9 million to $7 million.

The freighter still has five years remaining on its useful life, so Rio revises the straight-line depreciation for the asset to be $600,000 per year. This is calculated as the revised $7 million carrying amount minus the $4 million salvage value, divided by the five remaining years of the freighter's useful life.

Summary

Ship ownership is one of the most complex businesses in the world. It involves a dizzying amount of paperwork and tight monitoring of the economics of shipping to turn a profit, especially when the industry is going through one of its periodic oversupply bubbles. Having a good understanding of the accounting for ship owners can make a significant difference in whether the owner turns a profit, because it allows you to properly summarize and report on a massive number of revenues and expenses – any of which could mean the difference between a profit and a loss.

Glossary

A

Affreightment. A contract hiring a ship to carry goods.

B

Bareboat charter. When an owner hands over a ship to a renting party, who must hire a crew and operate the vessel.

D

Dead freight. The amount of money equal to the difference between the freight paid on the cargo actually loaded and what would have been earned if the ship had been fully loaded; this arises when the charterer does not fill the ship to the capacity stated in the charter agreement.

Demurrage. A charge payable to the owner of a chartered ship because of a failure to load or discharge the ship within an agreed-upon period of time.

Depreciation. The planned, gradual reduction in the recorded value of an asset over its useful life by charging it to expense.

Dispatch money. A charge payable by the ship owner to the charterer if a cargo is unloaded sooner than the agreed-upon time.

Dockage and wharfage. Dockage is the fee for berthing a vessel at a pier, while wharfage is the fee to use a wharf to unload cargo.

Dry-docking. When a ship is taken to a service yard for cleaning and inspection.

I

Intermediate survey. An inspection conducted between the second or third year between dry-docking, where the scope of the inspection depends on the age of the vessel.

T

Time charter. An agreement to charter a ship for a specific period of time.

Towage. When a tugboat pushes a larger ship.

V

Voyage charter. An agreement to charter a ship between two named locations.

Index